# Keyword Poetry

## Christian Crochet

BookLeaf
Publishing

India | USA | UK

Presentation by *BookLeaf Publishing*

Web: www.bookleafpub.com

E-mail: info@bookleafpub.com

ISBN: 9789357446907

First edition 2022

# DEDICATION

Dedicated to everyone giving me the three random keywords which are the base to the poems and the persons who inspired me to write about life and it's mysteries.

# ACKNOWLEDGEMENT

A big thank you to Eva, my mom, who encouraged me to write more poetry when I discovered it while taking a course about Text Analysis. Who is supportive and shares a big interest in the poems I write.

To my best friend Mitzy, giving me the courage and wisdom to pursue my dreams and making me accomplish more than I originally have within me, for the spot on advice you share for me and helping me grow immensely. Your magic humbles me.

To my university teachers who opened my eyes to the beauty and the wonderfully rich world of poetry.

A special thanks to Rowan, who pushed me to share my poetry out in the open and connect with those that are willing to listen and resonate with me.

To Lincie and Sam from Labyrinth holding the space and creating the stage for all the open mics you are hosting, making me shine through sharing and receiving poetry.

To my Labyrinth tribe, sharing your love and dedication to poetry and inspiring me to see and experience your world through poetry.

To all the lovely poets from Club House Vortex
Sutra: Eva, Nadia, JaeMar, Dirish, Ramsay,
Phyl, Anastasia and all the others.
To Yentl, dear fellow poet who's light shines
bright like gold and makes my inner child jump
of joy, I will never forget our creativity
combined together.
To Erika, who makes me feel more connected to
poetry, who listens to feel and teaches me to be
truly present and aware, you are wonderful.
To my housemates Natalia, Anke and Emil who
make time to listen to my poetry and share their
valuable insights on them.
A big thanks to The Poetry Class giving me the
opportunity to see poetry in a different way,
creating tools to hone my craft and to giving me
more understanding and insight on how poetry
can heal trauma and capture experiences and
memories in depth.

Finally, to all those who have been a part of my getting there: Joya, Iep, Francien, Sarajan, Charlotte, Dominic, Carmen, Amber, Dayo, Yorsalem, Ronja, Marleen, Mudinja, Kimberley, Esther, Hannan, Linda, Franske, Amandy, Saar, Sandra, Donna, Paul, Stacy, Jo Anna, Akorshi, Jesse, Miles, Miguel, Clarissa, Angel, Kevin, Coos, Stella, Jana, Lachlan, Alexander, Jayne, Angela, Lionel, Dila, Hei, Relinde, Kannakee, Edwin, Eva, Melody, Aylin, Yousra, Justine, Ariana, Gershwin, Emnée, Hélène, Bernadette, Linsey, Dorro, Eefke, Johanna, Lucille, Mireille, Mirjam, Saskia, Soufia, Sif, Tom, Vera, Matu, Fatima, Gina, Jurgen, Vivian, Suzanne and you reading this!

# PREFACE

First of all, thank you for getting this book, truly, it wasn't that easy to get here.
I had quite an adventure getting all the poems in this collection.
First of all, I had the thought of using only keyword poetry from others, may it be friends, family or complete strangers. As the deadline was nearing I noticed that I didn't have enough examples to fill this whole collection. What popped up in my head was to combine the keyword poems together with poetry I wrote myself. So now you can see the differences in writing. Besides this decision, the poems you're about to read are in English. In the future I will publish Dutch and French poems.

# Dragon-Commute-Purple

You see me as a traveler
Getting on, getting away
Never able to catch me, I dare say
Like light rays beamed upon palm
In foolish colourful disarray
Might it be green, yellow or purple
For you it's so easy, not even a hurdle
You laugh it away with mischievous glee
So I am momentarily blind, unable to see
Your hurt quickly recomposed
Or was it the drug badly dosed?
And there you were, jumping into the vast space
of your childlike imagination
Telling stories to ease my mind
I was surprised with what you find:

Living forests with leafs of fire, water and ice
Or something completely different
like rolling dice
May it be about talking deers, dogs or dragons
They miraculously made sense in a way
The path and route you did commute
Did quicken my heart to boot
Restarting it with mindful matter to consume
Whistling away my pains and doom!

# Minefield-Rain forest-Minotaur

My heart is a minefield
Within an enclosed garden sealed
Its gates semi invincible open for those who see
With their hearts and souls alike
But the blind still struggle putting up a fight
The clueless shut in like the Minotaur
Wandering aimlessly by each hour
They guide themselves to a craze
This mental rainforest, ought to be a maze
Ever flowing drop from leaf to leaf
From tree to tree, into the mossy grass
Rhythm serene, even this inquietude
Strays away in oblivion
You got to act now, your decision!

# Lampshade-Fridge handle-Tinnitus

In the club
Loud, sweaty and raw
One step closer and tinnitus is bound
Hearless I see others in this festive jungle
Emerge in the liquids toxic alike
Shaving off their dread and angst away
Not for me though, I am in control
Will not succumb to the false courage
I see within them, prancing around
But I'm not appalled nor dumbfound
I get it, this release, this escape
For others a way out, things they can't handle
May it be music, food a fridge handle far
Calm your addiction, you're not at war.
Get some rest, keep it cosy
In bed or sofa
The lampshade is your friend, I told ya!
You wouldn't listen
Too occupied in the story formed out of paper
Into your mind, with your smile on your lips
You devoured it all
Reading, you favourite drugs every fall

As we fall in the autumn of decision
Let me tell a story, perhaps my vision:

Of kids playing, while their parents are waiting
Waiting for the change that's about to fall
Fall into place. With no worry nor waste
Bypassing the borders of bipolar bigotry
The parents complain, the kids
still playing free
Free of discomfort any has felt
Where starry sun with nature's touch has melt
Melt away moved us closed to the Way
The way we see, feel and touch
Like the kids playing,
still fun to watch
Watch them with wonder instilled
Where creation flows free
Odd-worldly forced are willed
Willingly they come to be
Like kids playing
Like you
Like me

# River-Sound-Escape

Do you hear the wordful whispers
from paper unfold
About lives too many to count but told
These rivers of visions clearing your mind
As you see, they taught you a lot in hindsight
They helped you through hardships
ups and downs
Got you laughing, got you crying,
maybe of clowns?
We will never know, but one thing is true
It surely is a blissful escape for you!
Child of beauty and of wonder
Your soul light breaks asunder
You skin, into this world

Your creations flowing
From limbs, mouth and eyes alike
You best everything out of imaginable delight
Your presence freshly quickening all heart
Because you share it, your precious red shard!
Let it be heard, for you all this everlasting sound
Setting into your core
every time too many times to count
We are awake, let our lives begin
Steady, mindful and akin
To our purposes and beliefs
It will un encumber your life
Fast track away from the griefs
Lest you won't be sorry, jump down, dive
Into swirling opportunities in clearful reality
You'll be at peace: equanimity

# Elevate-Oak-Bicycle

When selecting your thoughts
Does it even cross your mind
I feel striped and ripened by the existence
No fathoms dwelling here inside nor around me
My eyes are lit up by the marks of your being
When do you see me whilst standing before me
Can I be full or empty ?
I dare do not say, for my whispers are deafening
Do you see me commuting in your brain with
the red bicycle you find childish
Or are you running my insides out
like a fast track to emotional success?
I will tell you, at the top there's nothing alike
Rest assured you will find spiritual release
Which will root and ground you
I am rooting for you
Like trees create life for humans

For I am an odd worldly oak
The kind that transgresses translations
All together we are one
Let you bloom from my waters soak
Into fruition we weep into form of water
As we elevate from Gaia's riches
We respond with our personal wishes
Of greed and whatnot
When do we realise we're fighting for naught?
Let us remember our lingering origin
And recreate the world without sin

# Curly-Dark-Piercing

How do we find ourselves?
Is it in the dark or the light?
Is it in clubs or bookshelves?
Or do we rather feel, without sight?
These feelings are genuine
But don't let the mind cover, shield it away
in disarray
Let instinct reign free, releasing dopamine
And sparkle, burst with piercing display
Full of curly inhibitions

# Nucleus-Dolphin-Phantom limb

Where do the waters flow from dolphin tears?
Are they as salty
as the sea they swim with peers?
Let these questions sink deep down
Beyond coral reefs
and profound human core beliefs
Let's question our accusations with a frown
Turning to center
without waving away the importance of bees
We can't truly live without
Even after stung we cry and shout
While their deaths don't worry us at all
Without concern our magnificence and
humankind will fall

Turn back to Earth with strong embrace
 But before that it's the natural order we'll have
to face!
This nucleus task of origin must come into being
Otherwise we'll be crippled
by phantom limb we're feeling
Out of the ordinary, ordinarily so
Let's give it back
with others united strong to go
Where we have never been before,
our souls calloused and sore
Of the menial mental work ahead
eyeless tears are shed
It is balance in flora and fauna we must set!

# Snow-Light-Cup

Your innocence is like white powdery snow
When we first met
Queen Winter reigned the night
Embracing Gaia one night with white
I felt vigor full of love and life
You being receptive to my mind
Turning and whirling around you
Like the blizzard outside
The one we did not see nor feel
Because the connection was warm and real
Dancing the night away
with no words on our lips we went part way
I knew your going wasn't goodbye
Feeling content without wondering why
We found each other where words meet
Where poetry is sung in unison beat
We feel and feed our drums closer

This calm serene bond deeper
Skin and flesh churning
Light trails burning
Unleashed from wildfire from the soul
This loving pain is not the goal
We are here for a large purpose to adhere
Let us co-create with intentions clear
Like winter's gift reflecting into the softness
Of your kindhearted eyes, behold
Your lush creek of boundless love
Feelings untroubled but bold
Aligned being oneness
Let me accept this cup my dove
Let myself empty before thee
This my jesting heart be filled
And now stronger power be willed!

# Rainbow-Stars-Flying

When I see you flying, soaring in the sky
Endlessly effortless gliding smile
I forget my troubles as fleeting goodbye
Peaceful at rest magnificent for a while
You are present in this time, slowly shifting
To the unforeseen truths up ahead and around
Experience and express them, truly sing!
The enchanting songs will help you ground
From there up you see the pretty stars
Align never obsolete they will find their way as
you shall too
Remember the lessons learned from scars
Old, dry, faint on the skin, what will they do?
Unmoving but confirming your life colours
Your rainbow palette as you may
Call them whispering indoors
Radiating the experiences hold dear to display
Shine so bright as you will
It is really kind and chill

# Love is

Love is:

She is.
No more
No less

# Words on People

In your eyes sparkle shine
you lift me up
make the world feel divine
cheers to that, fill me a cup
let's drink when the moon is rising
just banter away
into the morning lights
reading the words from you smile
about joys you care not say
don't let these moments fly
just harbor them for long while
unless you're gone, please stay
in you heart poured out
with willful play come shout
to others passing by
nonsensical utter delight
to unknown empty faces
going nowhere or to places
bewildered complexions what a sight

to behold and forgiven
in the present untold
of stories;their facial lines given?
wearing their history bold
chiseled or carved by
life itself experience
in utter complete bliss
amass sunshine from so high
soak it up, nothing amiss

colours dancing on my eyelids
telling sunny stories
of faraway places of wits
let them continue, un-decrease
the creases, the fatigue
giving you a joy you didn't seek
out-worldly destinations they come from
when they arrive they're done but some
keep going on
through your core, lightning the essence
radiating effervescence

# Blood Moon

How can I feel for you other than fully?
How can I see you other than clearly?
I don't want to break your heart by saying: I love
you
My fears are controlling me unfairly cruel
Why do I run towards my insecurities?
When I do know nothing grows there
Let us be in the life and light of sun's bright
Or your moon, your delight
Let me grow alongside our sorrows
For our tears will water down our walls made
internal
Our make-believe infernal place
For there is hope after all
As water the soft flow can crumble the sturdiest
misconceptions and dismal!
This one's for you my dear
Breathe, attune and align
It will free this irrational and rational fear

# Disconnection

I feel the nature blowing
Blowing through my fingers
Soft breezes are playing with my fingertips
My hair rested on soft pillows
My world is now unplugged
No sounds of the digital wind are present
They keep their distance
We are silent
We are not alone
The vastness of Mother Earth is all around us
Wilderness is pressingly omnipresent
Seeping in my being
I am aware
We are aware

# Origination

When I am
I am there
There where I culminate
2 lines intersecting
Creating me
2 origins converging
Creating me
2 descents ascending
Creating me
2 roots growing
Creating me
2 beginnings starting
Creating me
2 bloods mixing
Creating me
2 races running
Creating me

Do I agree
With this pedigree?
Does my lineage define me?
From birth I choose my parentage and my tribe
I do not care to oblige
Your curiosity in origin emanating
Let the poem talk, sing
Of tales widespread over the world akin
Slumber in depths of hearts rekindled
Let it be there, creep into the cracks of overawe
Where we pause and sit
Set it ablaze with our history in our gaze
We seek sanctuary in Souls tribe
Where music is received with moving bodies
Experience the precious present
Otherwise I just can't
Justify my reply to your question: why?
When I am
I am there

# Lab

I am an open book
For those who can read
the white words on the paper
There's a story to be unfold
About emotions run cold
In the heat of the moment
Bright, when eyes meet
And greet for umpteenth time
Full of spark and shine
Like shimmering dark coal
Sometimes amiss or whole?
Time won't tell for it's gone

# Love

Love


I am having a relationship with myself
But you are free to tag along, enjoy the ride
Share the love you have for yourself with me
Together we are as wonderful as alone
Don't you see?
That we are is all that matters in this moment
Everything is true, raw and pure
Forget all the preconceptions
Of what society seems right and wrong
We'll just play a tune and sing our song!
Life's melody with our beating hearts
Where our fingers articulate the soul-felt lyrics
Created spontaneous in here and now
Living day by day with no how
We end up, ever or never
It's not for us to decide
How time's tidings will go
Be aware and present in this flow

# Half past midnight

Intelligent intelligible words are sung
They moved me not, got careless stung
By them all or none
They were fleeting flying, gone
In and out of my ears, unheard of
Often found on blue pavements
Wondering carelessly aiming to amend
The golden woods out of you
Mirrored by my mystic me
Message this delay delayed distortion
To the pitch alternating between the two beats
Beats me how they do it
Sharp irrelevant irregularities
Demanding to work the rights to fees
Follow them, please thank them
The poetic practicing plastic cloves
Moment still. Captured flurred doves
Kicked off army boots taken by bedding
Sunken wet ocean sand and moved
Not nowhere to a standstill
While dreaming of his event going up hill
Ever going, showing the aces, the ancestral
climb
Up top, what a view, what a sight!

# Streams

When I see the streams of the mountains ahead
Still standing but moving through it all
I feel the airy vertigo rushing in awe
My insightful insignificance probably set
Loose on these stones my pebbles shake
Tumbling out my restless rêverie
I sat down just to settle and to meditate
To ground together truly felt free
Opening my core light to shimmer and shine
Embracing Earth laid bare under my feet
Giving me support reassuring every day
Catching us when we doubt, waver or sway
Taking a new step, opportunities for all to meet
Our lessons with persons, animals and plants
For they can all teach us, even the smallest ants
Of our strength slumbering inside
Which is limitless where none has to abide
To restant restrictions superimposed
Listen to your breath and heartbeat
It matters most!

# Flow

Even if we rhyme for less than a dime
We are rich without riches
Let's keep the Love of words alive
Let's keep the Word of Love alive
Ravishingly radiant we speak
Giving the world lessons on how to treat
Our kind with respect in each response
Keep it bountiful and not just once
For our words shapes truths whole
When we care to listen not by ear
yet through soul
We flow in the moment without stagger
Don't let it hurt like a dagger
But pierce you like mighty sword
While it strengthens your life cord!

# We do matter

As time has foretold
Soul-fires alike in this cold
Forming and binding
These joys deciding
Our luck ahead
Positively well fed
In comfort and play
We are to stay
Without a care in bed
reminiscing our future
Unborn but strong
That will fuel us, nurture
The teachings of right and wrong
Before we descend upon this earth
Before we are thrown into birth
Let us rejoice
This moment of vastness
After this decision, choice
We have made a mess

# Life on my 31st

When we fall
Into the fall
We become seasoned
Ripened by the years we lived
Where we cried
Where we loved
Where we were reckless
Where we were too afraid
Where we laughed tearfully
Where we experienced our first times
Where we mourned loss
Where we embraced the new
Where we experienced excitement
Where we felt alone
Where we felt held
Where we sweat
Where we slept peacefully
Where we had nightmares

Where we felt inspired
Where we felt utterly empty
Where we were in total bliss
Where we were enraged
Where we were engaged
Where we felt morose
Where we ponder
Where we took action
Where we gave up
Where we rested
Where we got tested

So my question to you:
Where are you at?